TINDER FAILS

TINDER FAILS

The most WTF? moments from the world's favourite dating app

Tom Phillips

sphere

SPHERE

First published in Great Britain in 2014 by Sphere

5 7 9 10 8 6 4

A CIP catalogue record for this book
is available from the British Library.

ISBN 978-0-7515-5973-6

Typeset in Helvetica by M Rules
Printed and bound in Great Britain by
Clays Ltd, St Ives plc

TINDER is the registered trademark of Tinder Inc

Papers used by Sphere are from well-managed forests
and other responsible sources.

 MIX
Paper from
responsible sources
FSC www.fsc.org **FSC® C104740**

Sphere
An imprint of
Little, Brown Book Group
Carmelite House
50 Victoria Embankment
London EC4Y 0DZ

An Hachette UK Company
www.hachette.co.uk

www.littlebrown.co.uk

To my colleagues, for being the best.

CONTENTS

INTRODUCTION

Online dating has come a long way from the days when it was a furtive, secret activity you hid from your friends and when arranging a date always felt like it had a strong chance of ending up with you getting kidnapped and held prisoner in a sex dungeon. It's now the norm, and has been for a long time – to the extent that there are now probably teenagers making dating profiles on the same websites their parents met on. (The venerable Match.com claims that over a million babies have been born to couples who met through their site.)

But, for all the explosion of niche sites and corporate behemoths, the basic online dating experience still hasn't changed a huge amount in that time. You fill out a profile, tediously try and find some way of describing yourself that makes you sound interesting, then try and find a connection with someone based on your shared love of beekeeping and Bulgarian folk music. You sit back, and wait for the messages that – mostly – never arrive.

Enter Tinder.

If you don't know Tinder, the idea is beautiful and terrifying in its simplicity. You sign up to the app. Taking its cue from the wildly successful gay app Grindr, it uses your location to show you a series of pictures of people of your preferred gender who are in roughly the same area as you. It skips the 'setting up a profile' stage by just grabbing pictures from your Facebook, and also tells you if you have any Facebook friends in common with that person. If you're not into them, you swipe left to reject them (they'll never know you did this). If you think there might be something there – it doesn't have to be much, no more than the internet equivalent of a second glance at a person across a crowded bar – you swipe right. You keep doing this, an addictive, rapid-fire burst of simple 'yes', 'no' judgements.

Ideally, in theory, what this does is create a grand, virtual version of all the parties that should happen but – in the real world – never will. Parties filled with single people from the same part of town as you, who you're already friends of friends of – but, crucially, without the looming shadow of potential rejection. Because that's the added advantage of Tinder: swiping right doesn't do anything unless that person also swipes right on you. Unless they're also up for that second glance – the online equivalent of meeting each other's gaze across that bar – they'll never know you were interested. There's no soul-crushing social fumbling to try and guess if somebody might just possibly be into you. Just swipe left, or swipe right. But if they've also swiped right on you, you get told that there's a match, and invited to start a conversation with them. Perfect.

This, of course, is where it can all go horribly wrong.

Because no matter how clever the algorithms that put people together (and Tinder, which is owned by the same firm that owns Match.com, doesn't even try to do the kind of smart matching that other dating sites do) at some point you have to actually talk to people. And that's when you discover that there is nothing weirder in the world than people desperate for a shag.

That's where this book comes in. All the conversations in here are ones shared by real people on the internet. (Names and identifying details have been changed to protect everyone's privacy/embarrassment.) Some are awkward. Some are unexpectedly cute. Many are utterly cringe-inducing. Lots of them are people trying out chat-up lines they saw on the internet, to varying degrees of success, and others are clearly just comedians trolling people so they've got a funny screenshot to share.

As with anything that involves the search for love

and sex, the Tinder experience isn't always a great one. You can often find yourself talking to trolls, to people who wildly overshare, to pornbots, or to someone from the skeevy 'pick-up artist' community, trying out tips on how to manipulate people into sex. (There was an entire potential section of this book called 'Men are terrible', which I left out because it was too dispiriting.)

But at the same time, it remains a weirdly compelling experience. Partly that's because, despite its simplicity, there are so many ways to use it. There are cultural differences; my colleagues in New York tell me that there it's predominantly a hookup app, used for casual encounters and avoided by people seeking serious relationships. In the UK, it seems be more a rapid-response triage system for winnowing down potential dates; a frantic, virtual version of speed-dating. And, of course, you can always just use it as a quickfire game of 'hot or not', because superficially judging complete strangers is always fun.

Ultimately, the lesson of Tinder is that, no matter how much the white heat of technological advancement changes the ways we try to find love, some things will always stay the same: people will remain awkward, freaky weirdos who probably shouldn't be allowed to tie their own shoelaces without supervision, never mind be allowed to rub parts of their body on parts of other people's bodies.

If there's one thing I've taken away from compiling this book, it's that you should probably abandon all hope right now. Upon no account should you ever try to form a relationship with another human being. Basically, never talk to people; ideally never leave the house ever again. Maybe get a cat? No. No. Getting a cat might involve interacting with other humans. That way disaster lies.

But for the people out there still willing to throw themselves into the madness of it all, who still have hope, who still think that some form of human connection might be possible amongst all the crackpots: I salute you. You are heroes of sex. You are brave adventurers sending back dispatches from the frontier of dating. I wish you all the luck and joy in the world. Also, um ... do you fancy a drink some time? Nothing serious, you understand. Just to get to know each other.

Hello ... ? Hello?

Oh.

THAT'S NOT A JOKE

So Claire, would you rather fight 100 duck sized Morgan Freemans, or 1 Morgan Freeman sized duck.

Oh, and the Morgan Freeman sized duck would narrate the fight in his soothing voice

👤 *If I flip a coin, what's the probability of me getting head?*

> *1 Yes, you think I'm endearing?*
> *2 Shall we discuss this?*
> *3 No you think Im a dickhead*

👤 I don't get it?

👤 Whats not to get?

👤 Well none of those are probabilities?

👤 *Think you're looking at this wayyy to literally. Lol*

🧑 *Hey! If we were the last 2 people on earth during the zombie apocalypse, would you be able to commit a murder-suicide for us in order to not be eaten?*

👤 *If you got stranded on a deserted island – and could only bring 1 thing. What would it be? And don't say a seat because that's what my face is for*

> 👤 Can I practice "negging" you?

> 👤 Do I even want to know what that means?? Lol

> 👤 It's when you attempt to dehumanize someone to make up for your crippling insecurities and garbage personality

> 👤 Idiot

> 👤 You in love yet

Hello

There are seven planets. I'm going to destroy your ass

No no you did it wrong. It goes: "there will only be seven planets after I destroy Uranus" but your logic is flawed because there are actually more than 8 planets. So I dunno. You wanna try that again?

Your missing the point. I just wanted to fuck you in the ass

Yeah I know but where's the intrigue?

I'm pansexual so I'm attracted to personality btw

I'm also pansexual and am attracted to pans

Oh so you date all genders and don't care about looks

But also pans

Why does Noddy have a bell on his hat?

No idea?

Cos hes a cunt

Right

No worries

Are you the gulf of mexico? Cuz I'd like to drill you and make a huge mess

... and then refuse to clean it up and blame it on some other guy

Wtf

👤 *I would drag my nuts through a mile of broken glass just to smell the exsaust fumes that came from the car that was driving your knickers to the cleaners.*

👤 *I'm in a huge dilemma right now. Can you pleeeaassee help me out?*

Brian, Carlos, Evan, Dana and Fara are trying to find seats in a movie theatre. Brian must sit next to Dana no matter what. Dana cannot sit next to Evan. Carlos must sit on Dana's right if Evan sits in the aisle. There must be one seat between Fara and Brian. If Brian sits in the aisle, would you sit on my face?

POINTS FOR TRYING

👤 *I just got pulled over by a cop writing my initial response. He gave me the whole "texting and driving is dangerous ... Blah blah blah" speech and was about to give me a ticket. But I showed him your picture and explained what Tinder was. He let me off with a warning and said I'd better get your number.*

👤 *What are your life aspirations?*

👤 To be resurrected like our Holy Father

Do you work at subway?

Insert joke about foot long. Am I right?

I was gonna say six inch . . .

Aye girl you like water?

is the pope catholic

Just say yes instead

yes

The you guaranteed to like 70% of me 😎

fuck off

Hello, I just saved a baby seal. What's up?

Just to inform you, I'm on the phone to iTunes customer service right now, they've made and error; you're the hottest single of 2014

Oh wow hahaha

I drew a graph of how well that opener went down

If you could dive into any substance what would it be?

vaseline

Sounds like a tight squeeze.

ha

Awful and tacky. I know.

its ok you tried

And not very hard.

wow ok

I'm horny

Hi horny, I'm Lucy

Smooth

Lol your hot

No, I'm Lucy

Hello, I am proficient In Microsoft Word.

This won't do, but thanks for trying.

🧑 *Can I go down on you for about 30 minutes, and take you out for a martini?*

🧑 Woah the martini part is way out of the question

🧑 *Cold beer?*

🧑 *That's a recent photo of me*

🧑 *Dig my hot bod?* 😎

Hey

Hey

What's up

Hi

Hey

Hi :-)

Hey :)

Wats up?

Nice hat lol

Thanks

Good talk

WHAT PEOPLE SAY ON TINDER VS. WHAT THEY MEAN

'Book lover':
I've read all of Dan Brown's work.

'Music fanatic': I will never shut up about what 'proper music' is.

'Film aficionado': I'll be really snobby about any films you actually like.

'Food devotee': I own a Jamie Oliver book.

'Travel enthusiast':
I've been to Barcelona. Twice.

'Fitness freak': I fill the dark, gaping void in my existence with fruitless sweating.

'Coffee lover': I'm a nightmare in the morning.

'Beer fan': I'm a nightmare in the evening.

'Wine connoisseur':
I'm a nightmare in restaurants.

'Gin enthusiast':
I'm a nightmare at closing time.

'Whisky fanatic': I'm a nightmare
the NEXT morning too.

'Tea drinker': I'm not a nightmare.
I'm just very dull.

'Ambitious': I'm a psychopath.

'Successful': I'm a rich psychopath.

'Driven': I'm a rich psychopath
who wants to be richer.

'Entrepreneur': I'm a psychopath
who will constantly blame you for the
fact that I'm not rich yet.

'Renowned': I'm a rich,
narcissistic psychopath.

'Award-winning': They give awards for
being a twat now, apparently.

'Opinionated': I spend my time leaving angry
comments on news websites.

'Forthright': I have no manners.

'I don't suffer fools gladly':
I think everybody is stupider than me.

'I speak my mind': I always say the first
thing that pops into my brain.

'Maybe I'm a bit *too* honest': Maybe I just
really, really like insulting people.

'Proud Labour supporter': I have lots of
opinions about rich people.

'Proud Tory': I have lots of opinions about
poor people.

'Proud UKIP supporter': I have lots of
opinions about foreigners and ethnic minorities
and gays and basically everybody.

'Proud Green': I will never shut up about kale.

'Proud Liberal Democrat':
Hi, my name is Nick.

'Happy-go-lucky': I usually try to get other
people to pay for my drinks.

'Bubbly': I'm probably drunk quite
a lot of the time.

'Vivacious': I'm probably drunk most
of the time.

'Fun-loving': I'm drunk all of the time.

'Party animal': I am being thrown out
of a club as I write this.

'Free-spirited': I HAVE TAKEN ALL OF THE
DRUGS.

'I love a bit of banter': I am annoying.

'My banter is great': I am extremely annoying.

**'You'll need to be able to keep up with my
banter'**: Nobody has ever loved me.

'I'm a bit of a Bantersaurus Rex':
I am a terrible person.

'I'm basically Bantonio Banderas':
I am one of the worst people in history.

'I'm the Archbishop of Banterbury':
I am literally Hitler.

'Looking for my Prince Charming':
I have unrealistic expectations.

'Looking for my princess': I have
unrealistic expectations and centuries of
patriarchy backing them up.

'Looking for Mr Right': Let's be honest,
you are probably Mr Wrong.

'Looking for that special someone':
Looking for anyone. Please. Help.

'Looking for someone to complete me':
I self-identify as a jigsaw puzzle.

'Looking for friendship': I am looking for sex,
but don't want to admit it.

**'Looking for friendship or whatever else
comes along'**: I am looking for sex.

'Looking for friendship, fun and flirting': I am
looking for a bit of casual, no-strings sex.

'Looking for fun times': I am looking for a massive amount of casual, no-strings sex.

'Up for new experiences': I am looking for casual, no-strings sex while dressed as Pudsey Bear in a lay-by on the A14 with a middle-aged man called Gerald filming us.

'I enjoy evenings in as well as evenings out': I like stuff.

'I like long walks and lazy afternoons on the sofa': I like stuff.

'I'm equally at home in a fancy restaurant or the local caff': I like stuff.

'I have eclectic tastes': I like stuff.

'I'm always looking for a new hobby': I like stuff.

'I'm up for a good time': I like stuff.

'I'm spontaneous': I don't really think things through.

'I'm adventurous': I'll get bored with
you after three months.

'I'm an adrenaline junkie': I did a bungee
jump during rag week this one time.

'I love to experience new cultures':
I did a gap year, you know.

'I'm pretty worldly': I relate all conversations
to my gap year.

'I'm an explorer at heart': Seriously I will
never shut up about my bloody gap year.

'I think of myself as a citizen of the world':
I order in Italian at Pizza Express.

'Good sense of humour': I sometimes laugh
at things! I enjoy the human laughter feeling.

'Great sense of humour':
I got Chandler in a 'Which *Friends*
Character Are You?' BuzzFeed quiz.

'Quirky sense of humour':
Hope you enjoy *Monty Python* quotes.

'Zany sense of humour': I will film myself farting in your face and upload it to YouTube.

'Twisted sense of humour': Hope you enjoy rape jokes.

'I'm a good listener': I've practiced nodding while thinking about football.

'I really connect with people': I've practiced nodding and hugging while thinking about what to have for dinner.

'I'm very empathetic': I've practiced nodding and hugging and looking a bit sad while thinking about re-doing the patio.

'I'm a shoulder to cry on': I've practiced nodding and hugging and looking a bit sad and making supportive noises while thinking about what you would look like without your clothes on.

'I'm intelligent': Our relationship will be defined by my ability to do the *Times* crossword faster than you.

'I'm well-read': I will constantly
drop references to obscure books into
our conversation, even though I only read
the Wikipedia summary.

'I'm well-educated':
Let me tell you my hilarious stories about
what we got up to at Oxford.

'I consider myself a rationalist':
I will try to settle every argument with the
words 'you're just not being logical'.

'I'm a bit cheeky': I will grab your arse
at inappropriate times.

'I'm very cheeky': I will grab other people's
arses at inappropriate times.

'I'm a bit crazy': I will show you my arse
at inappropriate times.

'I'm a bit naughty': I will show a really
large number of people my arse at
inappropriate times.

'I'm a very bad person':
My arse has its own YouTube channel.

'I'm just chilling at home':
I'm frantically looking through Tinder.

'I'm just having a quiet one': I am always
having a quiet one because I am lonely.

'I'm just relaxing with my dog':
If you don't love me, please love my dog.

'I'm just relaxing with my cat':
My cat will NOT be happy about me bringing
a strange person back home.

'I'm just hanging with my friends':
I secretly hate my friends and will ditch them
at the slightest excuse.

'I'm pretty toned':
If I concentrate very hard I can make my
beer belly disappear for like five seconds.

'I'm very fit':
I really like looking at myself in the mirror.

'I'm quite athletic':
I smell of sweat most of the time.

'I'm a bit of a fitness freak': I drink protein shakes like they're actually enjoyable.

'I'm ripped': I'm totally on steroids.

'I'm warm-hearted': I'll forward you pictures of sad kittens I've seen on Facebook.

'I'm affectionate': I'll forward you pictures of sad kittens I've seen on Facebook and suggest that we adopt them.

'I'm very loving': I'll literally send kittens to your workplace and won't think it's creepy.

'I'm generous':
I would very much like to buy your affection.

'I'm kind': I think I deserve some sort of extra credit for basic human decency.

"I'm a bit of a fitness freak." I drink protein shakes like they're actually enjoyable.

"I'm ripped." I'm totally on steroids.

"I'm warm-hearted." I'll forward you pictures of sad kittens I've seen on Facebook.

"I'm affectionate." I'll forward you pictures of sad kittens I've seen on Facebook and suggest that we adopt them.

"I'm very loving." I'll literally send kittens to your workplace and won't think it's creepy.

"I'm generous." I would very much like to buy your affection.

"I'm kind." I think I deserve some sort of extra credit for basic human decency.

DREADFUL
PROPOSITIONS

👤 *You can be Sarah Jessica Parker and I can be Kim Jong-Un. We are both together in the back of a Honda Odyssey Minivan. No one has clothes on and there is a jar of Nutella in one of the cupholders. What happens next?*

👤 Can I cover you in nutella?

My dick is wanted by the CIA, can I hide it in your ass?

👤 *I want to paint you green and spank you like a disobedient avocado.*

👤 Well, at least now I have the best tinder story of anybody ... Mad points for creativity, but I'm jetting off to Nopeville now.

👤 *Of anybody?? Darn*

👤 *Your face is like McDonald's*

Lets make sex.

How high are your results with that tinder line?

I've done the sex in three women from it. One might have been a man.

What do you say we go halfsies on a baby?

Isn't that how it usually works?

It's actually usually just me ... Flushing my dreams of having children right down the drain.

Literally.

👤 *Want to go halfsies on an abortion?*

👤 Has that line been working for you?

👤 *I mean I wouldn't say working? ... 10%?*

👤 That's a higher percentage than I would expect.

👤 *So you're a single mother of one?*

👤 *Yeah!!*

👤 *Want to be a single mother of two?*

👤 *Sit on my face and I'll eat my way to your heart.*

🛡 *Real talk imam eat da whole ass*

🛡 No thanks

🛡 *And that's just the appetizer*

If we play heads or tails, what's the chance of me getting head?

Slim

👤 *The names Jenkins, Alan Jenkins. You probably don't understand a word I'm saying, but I gotta tell you, you're the most beautiful women I've ever seen in my life. And I'd quite like to strip you down and butter you like a slice of wonderbread, and shave your armpits, and pour honey all over your naked body, and for the next 2 weeks pretend I was a hungry bear*

> **Would you be willing to refer to me as Eddard Stark under bedcovers?**

FINEAPPLE

If you're a fruit you'd be a fineapple

Nice one :) I have to remember this

Are you gonna steal it 😠

Yes :)

Soo are you gonna use it back on me?

Ok I'll take the silence as no

CAN I TAKE
THAT BACK?

👤 I'm not good at making the first move, or any moves for that matter. I would like to get to know you better and I hope you feel the same. So what's your favourite colour skittle?

👤 Mine is red, green used to be my favourite but they changed it from lime flavoured to green apple, it was very upsetting.

👤 I wouldn't want to talk to me either. Sometimes I just stop listening to what I'm thinking, but then I get very confused.

Hi Julia, I'm Greg, nice to digitally meet you! You are very pretty aesthetically.

My name is Jane ...

Have you ever sat there wondering what you're going to say to someone because you don't wanna be awkward and then you end up saying all of this?

Or nah?

My doctor says it's probably not contagious so we're good.

ooops wrong person. So what's up?

👤 *Hey :) :) :) :) :) :) :) :) :) :) :) :) :) :) :) :) :) :) :)*

👤 that was an inappropriate amount of smileys

👤 *Sorry I never know how many to do :/*

👤 oh ...awkward ...

👤 *:(*

👤 *Do you think that if two people made out hard enough they could switch brains?*

What's Liz short for?

Elizabeth lol

My guess was The Lizard King

Wanna know what my second guess was

Yes

Disney's The Lizard King

Come pver

Very strong introduction

👤 *You look like a chipmunk! ...I love chipmunks!*

👤 *I went too far with the chipmunk thing didn't i*

👤 *Aaaaaalvinnnnnn!*

I want to fuck you

hey***** omg autocorrect

Wowza

you do drugs at all?

👤 *I like your tits*

👻 You literally can't even see them in any of my pictures I don't understand

👤 *I'm assuming that they are nice*

TINDER PICTURES AND WHAT THEY MEAN

Picture of themselves with a drink: It's very unlikely you'll ever see me without a drink.

Picture of themselves with a friend: Let's play a fun guessing game as to which one of these people is me.

Picture of themselves with lots of friends: Here's a tip for the fun guessing game – the one you like the look of almost certainly isn't me.

Picture of themselves with a dog or a cat: This adorable animal will hopefully make up for the gaping flaws in my personality. Focus on the pet. FOCUS ON THE PET.

Picture of themselves from an unusual angle: This is literally the only angle from which I look human.

Picture that only shows their chest: Yeah, I'm probably not in this for a meaningful long-term relationship. But look: chest!

Picture of a man with a lion:
I want you to identify me with the lion. I want
you to think of something wild, untamed; a
noble yet savage beast just waiting to be
unleashed in all its majestic glory.

Basically what I'm saying is the lion
is my penis.

Picture of a woman with a lion: I like lions.

**Picture of themselves with a child in the
third world:** It's very important to me that you
understand that I'm a better person than you.

**Picture of themselves standing beside an
orphanage they helped build in the third
world:** It's very important to me that you
understand that I'm a better person than
anybody you have ever met. Give up now.

UNEXPECTEDLY AWESOME

👤 Your daddy must have worked at Ikea because you are put together nice.

👤 I, uh, got that pick up line from Moe Szyslak

👤 That's pretty interesting

👤 I need Amanda Hugandkiss

👤 I've always been a big fan of Hugh Jass

👤 And Homer Sexual

👤 Haha

👤 Also, I'm a pretty good man to hug and kiss

👤 *Do you like men with big cocks?*

👤 *Yes ;)*

👤 *Sorry I wasted your time.*

🧑 *Hey will you please come over and sit on my face so I can eat my way to your heart??*

🧑 Have you heard the good news that Jesus Christ is Lord and Savior??

Did you fall from heaven . . . ?

Because, have sex with me?

Sorry, didn't suffer a head injury during the fall.

👤 *Are you an angel? Because I'm allergic to feathers and it's a serious concern.*

👤 You probably shouldn't go near the decapitated duck outside my gate, then.

So we both find each other attractive. Let's skip this tinder nonsense and embrace the inevitable. What's your #?

Not a fan of dick pics

Neither am I, so I'm glad we got that out of the way.

I can't stand when I give a girl my number and all I get are pictures of her phallus

It's rude

👤 *What do we tell our parents about how we met?*

👤 *you saved me from getting hit by a cab?*

👤 *I sound pretty brave.*

👤 *Wanna go for a ride on my big green tractor?*

👤 We can go slow or make it go faster? Hahaha

👤 *Down to the woods and out to the pasture!*

👤 Hahaha! I could go on and on. That was a good start to the conversation.

👤 *Thank ya. I'm sure you've heard worse. Since we're talking about tractors, can I get your number?*

Tits or nah?

Nah.

Respect

WHAT PEOPLE'S FAVOURITE BOOKS SAY ABOUT THEM

Fight Club: I enjoy thinking about punching people.

Bravo Two Zero: I enjoy thinking about shooting people.

Pride And Prejudice: I love how Austen subtly dissects the social mores of . . . I'm just thinking about Colin Firth.

The Hitchhiker's Guide To The Galaxy: I self-define as 'the funny one'.

Eat, Pray, Love: Let me tell you about my #firstworldproblems.

The Lord Of The Rings: I think popping down to the shops is a heroic quest.

The 7 Habits of Highly Effective People: I like telling people they're doing things wrong.

The Very Hungry Caterpillar: I identify strongly with the caterpillar.

The Catcher In The Rye: I'm still a
grumpy teenager at heart.

Harry Potter: I never grew up properly
(but I'm probably quite nice).

To Kill A Mockingbird: I bloody
hate mockingbirds.

WHAT PEOPLE'S FAVOURITE FILMS SAY ABOUT THEM

Titanic: I really like Celine Dion and weeping.

Garden State: I am emotionally stunted and cannot deal with real humans.

Monty Python and The Holy Grail: Hope you like *Monty Python* quotes, because that's the only way I can communicate.

The Shawshank Redemption: Going out with me will be like being in prison and you'll want to escape.

Anything with subtitles: I desperately want you to know how clever and cultured I am.

Save the Last Dance 2: I have good taste.

Tremors: YESSSSSSSSSSS.

JUST PLAIN WEIRD

👤 Were you named after a Pokemon?

👤 I don't think so lol

👤 Close enough, now I must weaken you until you almost faint and then! Only then! Can I trap you in a small container and use you to fight my battles!

👤 Umm ok lol

A wild Janet appears.

Brian uses Pick-up line.

That was horrible lol

Janet evades the attack and uses Play Hard to Get.

Brian uses Charm.

Janet leaves the playing field.

Brian continues to be weird.

How do you feel about antique dolls?

I prefer them headless

But then they can't watch.

👤 *I would run a 10 mile marathon with 20 pound weights strapped around each ankle with a small Asia man strapped to my back shouting insults at me while whipping the back of my head while a midget on a moped follows me with a paintball gun that's firing off rounds of frozen paintballs at my nether regions only to be greeted by a pack of wild hyenas that I will have to kill with my bare hands blindfolded just to shake hands with the janitor that cleaned your high school classroom at the end of it all.*

I don't have much time so just listen. I'm from the future, and in the future, the sex machines have taken over. They've sent a terminator back in time to orgasm you to death. Cum with me if you want to live.

👤 Jessie, you look like a very attractive nice girl. I want to be honest with you. My penis is usually referred to as an "one inch warrior" and I have moved back in with my mum. But, I am in town until Thursday and if you wish to enjoy 2 solid minutes of mediocre sex then get back to me.

what's your race

Skeleton

I hate you so much

I don't feel

I am a skeleton

Shit

FINEAPPLE 2

👤 *If you were a fruit you'd be a fineapple*

👤 Lamest pick up line I think I've ever heard hah

👤 *Hahah!!*

👤 *Well about that line uh ... Let's forget that :(What's your #?*

👤 How old are you? Haha

SHOT DOWN

SHOT DOWN

Hey how's it going?

What's up cutie

EWWWW don't say cutie

*majestic princess

Tell me a joke otherwise you go to block city

Hey Kelly, quick question: do you like apples?

no how do you like them apples?

Aw shit.

That was a very serious combo breaker for the rest of that cheesy pickup line.

Your not much fun

Crap banter

Rude much

Honest though haha give me your best line

—— ———— —— —

How do you feel about anal?

I mean I prefer the term "perfectionist" or "obsessive compulsive", but whatever floats your boat.

👤 *Does it bother you when you see a man as good looking as me and you think "Damn why can't I have something like that as my own"?*

👤 Well actually I do have something like you on my own. But better looking :) and not a douche! Thanks though keep up the confidence

> 👤 *Hey Frances let's tell a story together! Once upon a time . . .*

>> 👤 you tried to think of a cool tinder line and couldn't think of one?

>> 👤 lol

I love your dress!

Are u gay?

Hey wanna grab a drink?

Hey uhhhhh look ... I'm not really into guys that look like they might wanna finger a lizard in their spare time..

I don't think this will work out

Were you raised on a farm?

Cus you sure know how to raise a cock

Too forward?

Actually I did grow up on a farm & was taught to strangle the cocks that got too out of line.

I'm getting mixed signals. Should my cock be in line or out of line?

Do you like raisins?

No, not even dates.

Fuck you

Your like my pinky toe. I'm going to bang you on my coffee table later.

Oh cool, you're like my pinky toe in that you're completely useless, irrelevant, and evolution will probz be weeding you out sooner or later.

What kind of dog is that

It's a kangaroo you fucking retard

Nudes

And I thought you'd be cool

Did you know they call my nob the hogwarts express xx

and whys that then

because its 9 nd 3 quarters ;)x

cm obviously, not inches

AWKWARD
SILENCES

Hey princess

What would I have to say for you to allow me to dig up your nan and bang her

sorry autocorrect lol

***take you for a drink**

Well hey there!

Can I eat nutella off you?

👤 *Are you an archaeologist? Cus I've got a bone that needs inspecting :) x*

👤 *yea. I never expect it to work either. Personally can't see why, seems a pretty solid chat up line to me?*

do you wanna have a Lotta sex with me?

okay I didn't even try. That was so bad I'm sorry I made you witness that.

but still have sex with me

Was your mother a beaver? Because DAAAAMN girl.

Oh. And I thought that was clever. Should have stuck with the tried and true.

I'm high and have a bone to pick

"I like people and fun"?

Everybody likes fun

Man that shit ain't a characteristic

Good day

If a train leaves Delaware travelling 74mph at the same time as another train leaves San Francisco travelling 61 mph

How long will it be until you talk to me?

👤 *2 fingers or 3?*

👤 *for when ur bowling*

👤 *yo . . . laura . . .*

👤 *what's poppin*

👤 *where'd ya go I miss you*

Hey you seem fun we should meet up to get a pizza and fuck

I guess you're not a fan of pizza?

I wana to see ur chest!!!

Yes or no

Babe :(

I'm hornu

Can I see ur boobs please

👤 I see you're a golfer

👤 I went mini golfing a few weeks ago and I was only 88 strokes over par, so I guess you could say I'm on my game with it

👤 This is going very well. Should we have chicken or beef at the wedding

TINDER: EXPECTATIONS VS. REALITY

Expectation: You'll immediately hit it off with a friend of a friend of a friend who you never knew existed but is actually a perfect match with you.

Reality: You'll keep swiping right on people who are already vague acquaintances, because you don't want to be rude, and then keep having really awkward conversations.

Expectation: You'll have a great time flirting with a wide range of people who are up for fun with no strings attached.

Reality: The first person you talk to is already planning your wedding after two messages, and the next thing you know you're meeting their parents.

Expectation: You will enter a wild and hedonistic world of unlimited sexual debauchery and carnal abandon.

Reality: You will still be at home alone with your cat on a Friday night, but now you'll be looking at Tinder.

Expectation: You'll finally discover a medium in which you can converse with people freely and easily, your natural awkwardness in social situations dissolving, allowing you to blossom into the witty and charming person you always knew you were inside.

Reality: AWKWARDNESS TIMES 100

Expectation: People will look like their profile photos if you meet up with them on a date.

Reality: Nope.

Expectation: People will look *better* than their profile photos if you meet up with them on a date.

Reality: A whole world of nope. Nope city. The last train to Nopesville. *Star Wars Episode IV: A New Nope.*

Expectation: You're just going to casually try Tinder out for a bit, but it's no big deal – you're not going to let it dominate your life.

Reality: A week later you're up at 3 a.m. desperately swiping left and right in search of The One.

Expectation: You're going to treat it all as a big game, and not let any rejections get to you, because that would be silly.

Reality: A week later you're up at 4 a.m. crying and eating ice cream while screaming 'why? WHY DON'T THEY LOVE ME? AM I SOME KIND OF MONSTER?!?' into the uncaring void.

Expectation: You'll get to try out all the super awesome, success-guaranteed chat up lines you read about on the internet.

Reality: Everybody you try the chat up lines on has already heard them seven times from other people, and they spelled them better.

Expectation: You'll meet loads of naturally funny, empathetic people you'll be able to really bond with during long, honest chats.

Reality: Everybody is just trying out chat up lines they read on the internet.

Expectation: You'll finally find someone to truly connect with over your deep love of *Monty Python* quotes.

Reality: First, you'll find another 647 people who don't really appreciate your *Monty Python* quotes in quite the way they should.

Expectation: Your long quest to find someone who's also into beekeeping, flamenco guitar and dressing in a realistic wolf costume during intercourse will finally be over.

Reality: You'll find a wolf-fetishist beekeeper who HATES flamenco and all your dreams will crumble to dust.

Expectation: You'll find a guy who is sensitive, caring and yet incredibly macho, whose perfect sculpted abs and world-beating pecs are only matched by the subtle insights of his poetry and the awesome power of his global multi-billion dollar internet start-up, who as a point of principle refuses to orgasm first no matter how horny he is.

Reality: You'll find a guy who still lives with his mother who wants you to send him pictures of your rude bits.

Expectation: You'll find a girl who is beautiful, sweet and caring, smart and funny in equal measure, with her own career and aspirations who won't sacrifice her dreams for anybody other than – perhaps – her perfect soulmate, who is yet astonishingly dirty in bed and is unexpectedly keen on enthusiastically administering oral sex at the drop of a hat.

Reality: You'll find a girl who just wants someone to frig her off behind a Wetherspoons in her lunch hour and buy her unlimited Bacardi Breezers.

Expectation: You'll hook up with someone who just wants quick, dirty, fast anonymous sex that brings you both to the absolute peak of ecstasy and then lets you walk away, the knowledge of your transgressive behaviour lending a glorious thrill to the whole encounter.

Reality: You'll get stuck in a very sad discussion about how someone's puppy just died.

Expectation: You'll just meet someone normal. Someone normal and safe and not bad-looking who wants roughly the same things out of life as you do and is willing to share that life with a fellow lost soul.

Reality: LOL.

OVERSHARE

👤 *Tracy let me cut to the chase. There's two ways we could do this: 1. I could ask you on a date, we would go out for a lovely romantic meal. It would be slightly awkward at first as we met on tinder but once you realize I'm a funny charismatic guy you soon relax into my company. From then on things would go smoothly. Frequent dates progressing into a relationship, we would love and laugh and generally enjoy each other's company. Eventually I pluck up the courage and ask you to marry me. We move into our first house. After falling pregnant you quit work and I take over the financial responsibilities myself.* ➡

Not long after the second child comes along and things start going downhill. You let yourself go an only have time for the kids, I'm working long hard hours to pay for the family and love leaves the relationship. I start an affair and my stupidity and bad lying leads to you finding out. Divorce. You get the kids and we agree that I can see them at weekends. The poor children then grow up with parents that hate each other. That's not fair on them, which brings me to item 2: we have a quickie, use a johnny. Everyone wins. Think of the kids Tracy . . .

I have cancelled my flight. Currently stranded and stunned by the euphoria you've struck my heart with. I am making arrangements for a our candle light dinner tonight and I'm lighting my suitcase on fire in representation of beginning my new life with Johanna, the love of my life. We will one day deadlift on muscle beach and we will get a post-workout fuck at a slum in the projects with snoop dogs relatives observing via binoculars. We will name our babies after the ninja turtles and even then their names won't live up to their heroic personalities. ➡

We will divorce abruptly but by that time I will have clapped you cheeks so many times that sex will be like throwing a corn dog in the Grand Canyon and completely undesirable for you. I will move on to slay new pink tacos but don't worry because for the present time, the love is real. See you in 26 minutes at Chipotle baby <3

👤 *Just wanted to say I find you very attractive. If I got to know you I would invite you over for a very romantic dinner and as soon as you arrived I would pull you close and whisper in your ear "I have a Swanson TV dinner in the fridge with yur name on it" and then proceed to fill a wine glass with with the finest grape juice welches has to offer …*

👤 How has that line worked out for you?

👤 *I was hoping if we hit it off in our messages then I could invite you over for a nice seafood dinner. I would catch lobsters myself with my bare hands from the nearest foreign waters that inhabit them, which would be the nearest red* ➡️ lobster down the street. I would then begin to cook them for you.. Naked if u desire. Then we would indulge in the lobsters and any other side dishes u would like as well as as sip wine that was fermented from my private vineyard on the grounds. Over dinner we would hit chat a bit, you could discover that I am more than just a guy with the physique of a Greek god, and I could discover that you are a smart heavenly blessed beauty just putting on a calloused face. If you enjoy my company then perhaps we could do it again, if not then you leave with a stomach of good food when otherwise on a night like that you would throw one of you lean cuisines in the microwave and watch Oprah.

What's the longest you've ever gone without showering? Because I'm at 27days and no one has said anything ...

👤 Sorry Siobhan, I was hoping for a reliable 6 or even 7 when dressed up. You're at least an 8 maybe even a 9 in your first picture. How would I ever get to sleep when laying beside you? I'm sure I'd be trying to ride you all the time! I wouldn't get a wink of sleep, then I'd lose my job and wouldn't be able to provide for our kids. I'll start drinking and lose my charming good looks, and then you'll have an affair with some guy from work who isn't the best looking but is a great listener. So, for those reasons, I don't think it would work.

Hey stacey! I'm Jeff. I like legs. Yours are nice. I'm an Aquarius, but I wish I was a Pisces. I once bowled a 100 free from performance enhancing drugs. I partied hard last night with no regrets throwing back 13 bud lights and 6 shots of fireball. I don't watch smut but I do enjoy taking ecstasy and dancing around naked in front of my cat while listening to Cher. Wanna get to know each other?

FINEAPPLE 3

If you were a fruit you'd be a fineapple

Well you're just a fruit

Ouch.

PINEAPPLE 6

If you were a fruit you'd
be a pineapple

Well you're just a nut

Ouch.

TERRIBLE
CHAT-UP LINES

I'm looking for a stud. I've already got the std, all I need is u

yikes! I'm not sure you ever want to open with the having an std part hahahaha

Haha I know. It was the only pickup line I could think of! Obviously I don't use pickup lines very often. And to clarify, I don't have an STD.

👤 *I just read your profile and you're like one of those elves in that tree ... except you're in my brain*

👤 *We should mate*

👤 *I don't know what you're saying*

👤 *That we should mate*

Sit on my face

I'd rather not

Well I tried my best

Alright

🧑 *Fuck me if I'm wrong but do u ever take ur tampon out and suck it?*

If you had 40 minutes to blow up the moon how would you do it

I'd be willing to bet you have a really nice clitoris.

That's a pretty weird thing to open with.

👤 Lets cut to the chase quickly. I just want to wear you around as a skin suit and nothing more.

Are you a terrorist? Cause you're smuggling bombs in your shirt

Fuck you

You have huge cans

👤 *You're worth missing a merseyside derby for aren't you?*

IT'S MEANT TO BE

I'm a pilot and small business owner. What do you do?

I fuck pilots and small business owners for a living.

What a match!

👤 Puppies! I 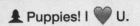 U.

🐶 *Woof!*

👤 here boy!!

🐶 *<pant>*

🐶 *Woof! Woof!*

👤 Let me scratch behind your sweet baby puppy ears.

🐶 *<wag><wag>*

🐶 *Arf!*

👤 Let's go solve crimes, Puppies.

🐶 *<scratches ear>*

♟ I'll get you a tiny bullet proof vest.

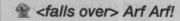 <falls over> Arf Arf!

♟ Aww, you distract the criminals with your cuteness and I'll sneak up behind them to slit their throats.

I'll just go straight to it. Do you want to have sex with me?

I already did

Let's quit our jobs ...

And drive off into the sunset?

How about we both enroll at Phoenix University and get degrees in marketing and then go work at McDonalds the rest of our life

👤 *You and I are locked in a room for 24 hours. We have; a jar of strawberry jelly (seedless), a jar of organic almond butter from Whole Foods, a Twister mat, a shower with a removable shower head, and of course the Titanic on Blu-Ray. What happens next?*

👤 Well my first instinct is to burn the almond butter because fuck almond butter and use the twister mat as a shower curtain. I feel like you intended this to be sexy or something but my mind is turning it into a survival situation.

Want to get weird?

I already am

Prove it

I speak Klingon

yeah that's pretty weird

Can you talk dirty in Klingon?

Klingon is a dirty language

Just ask star fleet

You're really cute!

I know

Hey! What's up?

Shalom

It's that obvious I'm Jewish? Haha

Did you go to jacob goldberg's bar mitzvah I must have met you there

Which jacob goldberg???

We each probably know like 5

When to we jump into sexting?

Right now, go.

Oh man I like this. No text foreplay needed tonight. Things are getting real

I am very efficient.

Are you aroused yet?

Already came.

Oh thank god. I didn't want it to be awkward if I came before you. Whew. Glad to get that out of the way.

In the name of Robert of the house of Baratheon, first of his name, king of the Andals and the first men, lord of the seven kingdoms and protector of the realm, I, Eddard of the house Stark, Lord of Winterfell and warden of the North, sentence you to send me nudes.

You are by a huge amount my favourite person on this planet right now

CLASSIC MOVIE ROMANCES THAT WOULD HAVE BEEN RUINED BY TINDER

FOUR WEDDINGS AND A FUNERAL

INT. WEDDING MARQUEE. AFTERNOON.

[CHARLES and TOM are at a wedding reception. CHARLES is on his smartphone.]

TOM: Blimey, Charles ... have you seen that American lady over there?

CHARLES: Uh. Hang on a sec.

TOM: Gosh, I think she might be looking at you. You should ... you know, er, do your ... talking thing.

CHARLES: Not now, Tom. One of the bridesmaids is on Tinder and I just told her that if she was a fruit she'd be a fineapple. I'm so in there.

CASABLANCA

INT. RICK'S, CASABLANCA. NIGHT.

[RICK is standing behind the bar, casually flicking through Tinder. SAM is noodling on the piano. RICK reacts with a start to his smartphone screen.]

RICK: Oh ... oh man, I just found my ex on Tinder.

SAM: You two still friends?

RICK: It's ... it's complicated.

SAM: Swipe left, dude.

RICK: Damn right.

[RICK swipes left and returns the phone to his pocket.]

WHEN HARRY MET SALLY

INT. SALLY'S APARTMENT. NIGHT.

[SALLY is on Tinder. A picture of Harry comes up.]

[SALLY swipes left.]

THE TIME
TRAVELER'S WIFE

CLARE: Hmmmm. You looked a
lot younger in your Tinder picture.

ETERNAL SUNSHINE OF THE SPOTLESS MIND

[JOEL and CLEMENTINE are sitting a few rows apart on a train to Montauk.]

JOEL: (Voiceover) That girl ... she looks ... familiar. I wonder if she's on ...

He takes his smartphone out of his pocket.

JOEL: (CONT.) Oh, wait. She's already a match ... hang on. We've got a really long chat history from like two years ago. Uh ... WTF?

BRIEF ENCOUNTER

INT. TRAIN STATION. EVENING.

*[We hear the noise of frantic copulation
in the train station toilet.]*

TITANIC

INT. BAR NEAR DOCKS, SOUTHAMPTON.
AFTERNOON.

*[JACK and FABRIZIO have just won a pair
of tickets on board the Titanic.]*

FABRIZIO: Come on, Jack!
The boat is almost about to leave!

JACK: I, uh . . . I kind of arranged a date
tonight with this chick I've been chatting to
on Tinder. You maybe want to ask Barry if
he'd like to go instead?

BROKEBACK MOUNTAIN

EXT. THE MOUNTAIN. DAY.

*[JACK is waving his phone around in the air.
In the background are many SHEEP.]*

JACK: Dammit. No signal.

HER

[Tinder also becomes sentient, and starts
bombarding SAMANTHA the operating system
with bad chat up lines it read on the internet.
SAMANTHA self-destructs before THEODORE
gets a word in edgeways.]

ANNIE HALL

EXT. NEW YORK. DAY.

[ALVY is talking to the camera.]

ALVY: There's an old joke – um ... two elderly women are at a Catskill mountain resort, and one of 'em says, 'Boy, the food at this place is really terrible.' The other one says, 'Yeah, I know; and such small portions.'

Well, that's essentially how I feel about Tinder – full of douchebags, and weirdos, and awkwardness, and people who are really keen to see nude pictures of you or to ask you to sit on their faces ... and it's all over much too quickly.

IT WAS ALL GOING
SO WELL

> 🧑 Do you think love is a real thing?

> 🧑 I think that's the beginning of an interesting conversation. You first.

> 🧑 I don't think anything is real. Everything is a construct of my diseased mind

> 🧑 I am alone inside my head

> 🧑 Want to get coffee?

Hey wanna come over and watch some porn on my flat screen mirror?

hahaha just for that comment, yes.

It will be premature ejaculation disappointed woman genre

Oh ...

I'm just kidding it's fine

Just very very tiny

So how bout it then

My neighbor Gary won't stop asking me to turn down my music. Any ideas?

Tell him to fuck off and crank it louder.

I meant ideas for murdering Gary

Yes, I have a daughter

That's cool. What's it like having a mini-you?

It's pretty awesome lol

have you taught her any cool tricks?

Wtf she's not a dog lol

How old is she?

3

It's not too late

What kind of pickup line would you like? Corny, or really corny?

You can give it to me however you want

Fast and disappointing?

You're my type of girl

I was talking about the pickup line you sick cunt

Just hanging with my bestie. How about you.

Same haha I'm currently in bed with my puppies

That's cute, what kind of puppies do you have?

Goldens!

How old are they? My dog just died. It got hit by a car and dragged 20 blocks

I really like how your finger is touching your nose in your profile picture.

You do?

Yeah it brings me back to the days where I could do that. One year I went to the Zoo like I had plenty years past and when I arrived there was a space samurai who went crazy and chopped my nose and my dick off.

Wow that sucks. Must stink not being able to smell

WOW YOU BIG DUMB IDIOT. SPACE SAMURAIS AREN'T AT THE ZOO, THER ARE IN SPACE. YOU ARE SO DUMB OMG LOL.

199

Meth. Yes or no?

No

Ughhhh. We aren't gonna work.

Guess not

👤 *Something tells me you are not celebrating Easter today?*

👤 Hail satan.

👤 *Well there's that ... but I was more hoping you were a jew?*

I LOVE your clothes

Haha thanks! :)

Down to ride my cock?

How tall r u?

6 foot 8

Wow ur pretty tall

Yeah some girls like it

But it sucks because I have really long legs and arms and big feet but tiny hands so when I run I look like a goblin sometimes

You there?

... down with Gerald.

I would def be Harold from the bar mitzvah episode

I'm not familiar, I honestly haven't watched Hey Arnold in like 10 years unfortunately

Haha super understandable

Yep

Tight

THIS IS GOING SUPER WELL 💩💩💩💩💩💩 💩💩💩💩

MISSION ABORT

👤 *Ur names is spelled unique. That must mean your tits are phenomenal . . .*

👤 *Get that from urban dictionary?*

👤 *No I was thinking of something that would throw you off . . . yet subtly romantic. Did it work or no?*

👤 *Umm no*

👤 *Dang.*

What's good Chill bi guy here. Not a fag or anything, I act like a dude.
Wondering if you'd be into getting some good head sometime. Would stay between us cause I date girls also. You don't have to do anything back, just sit back and relax, and you'd be in control of whatcha want me to do. Hit me up if you're interested in discussing a deal

Only if I get to cum in your nose

> **Hey beautiful what would it take for u to sleep with me**

> **Not going to happen**

> **How.bout a date? :P**

> **Not a chance now**

> **How bout 500$**

> **Go away**

What's good sexy

Hmu to fuck

Hmu to smash

You fat ugly bitch. You look like a fucking whale ... They made tread mills for a reason

That escalated quickly

👤 I see you're a fan of Desserts Delivered Susan!

👤 Not that you look fat, it's just come up as a shared interest

👤 This has gone badly

👤 Taxi!

Where you at? I wanna spoon feed you peanut butter

I'm allergic to peanuts x(

You are cute as hell, do you like to have fun?

So much fun

What kind of fun may I ask?

Netflix

How many tickles does it take to make an octopus laugh?

8, most likely.

Ten tickles

Why ten

TENTACLES!!! YOU GOD DAMN MOTHER FUCKIN STUPID PIECE OF SHIT!!!

Alright let's get the party started am I right?!

Yikes

I got a bottle of wine

A blanket

And a documentary on how canoes are made

Lets

Fucking

Do this!

FINEAPPLE 4

👤 *If you were a fruit you would be a fineapple ;)*

👤 If you were a fruit you would be an unORANGEinal. Because I've heard that line before. 🔥🔥🔥🔥🔥

IF MUSIC BE THE FOOD OF LOVE

Hey

I just met you, and this is crazy ...

Haha how so?

Damn, you ruined it.

Sorry. Let's start that again ...

Hey

I just met you, and this is crazy ...

Don't fail, don't fail

👤 *So, shall we skip straight to the important stuff? Tell me, what's your favourite Justin Timberlake song?*

If you could set fire to the rain will it stop? It's cold outside.

Not a fan of Adele jokes? It's ok. I didn't want someone like you anyway.

I could try but it would just evaporate, then condensate, then we'd just be rolling in the deep

hahah OK

Ok that's all the Adele songs I know. What's your stance on fisting?

Dec 24, 2013, 3:26 PM

👤 *You're all I want for Christmas*

Dec 26, 2013, 3:11 PM

👤 *You ruined Christmas*

Hey.

I'm only in town for 7 Days, how about we Rendezvous (everything I know about women I learned from Craig David)

Why, where are you going?

I'm walking away.

So what's your Flava?

Oh dead

**dead

Dear . . .

➡

👤 *Great typing. You were Born To Do It. :)*

👤 Broke my wrist a couple if months ago ... still a bit temperntal

👤 *Errrr. Looking through the Craig David discography. There is nothing on this*

👤 Awkssss

👤 He's not written sings on relevant thingzo

👤 *Ok I got this* ➡

How did you break your wrist? Fill me in.

Snowboard racing on a dry slope

Ah, the Rise and Fall.

...yeah?

Why are you 37 km away? Where do you love?

*live....

Live

😕

Craig David was born in Southaptom in 1981.

But I (Rhys) am in Hertfordshire.

Where are you?

Camden.

Ah, of course. ➡

It's Hypnotic.

What is?

Camden. With the Fast Cars. Time To Party!

Uhh

Just My Imagination?

Yes?

Prob

Ah. My bad. Rewind.

It can be exciting ➡️

It's great. I was just doing Craig David titles.

Oh

He's not even good

Pls stpp

That's not the point.

Ermmmmmmmm what's your point then?

Gender issues.

Sad times

👤 *Ha sorry I'm just messing around.*

👤 Yeah I gathered you've been messing around the whole conversation . . .

👤 *I actually work for Craig David's marketing team and we're trying to see if he's still popular with certain demographics.*

👤 Lol

👤 What's the outcome of this then? ➡

You will not be added to the Craig David mailing list.

Thanks

For this pointless conversation

'Pointless Conversation' is the title of Craig David's upcoming single! Congratulations, you have been added to the official Craig David mailing list.

Ffs

ACKNOWLEDGEMENTS

Thanks to Luke Lewis (my editor at BuzzFeed UK), Rory Scarfe and Jonathan Harris at Sport & Artist, and Hannah Boursnell and Rhiannon Smith at Little, Brown, who all conspired to make writing this book an implausibly painless and enjoyable process. Due to their combined efforts, I now have entirely unrealistic expectations about how the publishing industry works.

The Craig David conversation that closes the book was the work of stand-up comedian Rhys James (@rhysjamesy) – big thanks to him for letting us reprint it.

Both thanks and apologies are due to my friends and colleagues, who had to put up with me being all 'oh no I can't possibly do that I've got a BOOK to write because I am very important and fancy' for too long. Special thanks to Flo Perry for help in finding some of the conversations, and to Kate Arkless-Gray, Damian and Holly Kahya, and Kelly Oakes for reminding me to stop dicking about and actually write the damn thing.

And, of course, thanks to the internet for consistently being weird and astonishing. To all the people who shared their awkward Tinder moments with the world: good work. Keep it up.